Refusing to Quit

Key Principles to Overcome Life's Challenges

All rights reserved. No part of this publication may be reproduced, distributed, or transmitted in any form or by any means, including photocopying, recording, or other electronic or mechanical methods, without the prior written permission of the publisher, except in the case of brief quotations embodied in critical reviews and certain other noncommercial uses permitted by copyright law. For permission requests, write to the publisher, addressed "Attention: Permissions Coordinator," at the address below.

S.A.B Global Enterprise, LLC
1918 Shady Oaks Ct Missouri City, TX 77489
www.refusing2quit.com

Ordering Information:

Quantity sales. Special discounts are available on quantity purchases by corporations, associations, and others. For details, contact the publisher at the address above.

I dedicate this book to my Mother, Julia Ann Ball. You have and will always be my first example of what it means to never give up. I have watched you navigate some very tough obstacles, and you have always Refused to Quit on yourself, your kids, & your life.

I love you.

Contents

Acknowledgement vii

Forward ix

Refusing To Quit Introduction xi

Key Principle # 1: Acknowledge the Pain 1

Key Principle #2: Invest in Yourself and Your Healing 12

Key Principle #3: Understanding
                    Your Value 15

Key Principle # 4: Focus on the Positive 24

Key Principle #5: Identify Your Gifts 27

Key Principle #6: Have a Plan of Action 36

Key Principle # 7: Differences Between Success and
                    Failure is Consistency 49

Key Principle # 8: Be Prepared 60

Key Principle # 9: Define Your Own Success 64

Key Principle #10: Understand Yourself 74

About the Author 85

Acknowledgement

First, I want to thank my amazing husband, Zackery Emerson. You saw something in me that oftentimes I didn't even see in myself. You supported my vision, and I know you are truly my gift from God.

To my children: Grant and Kingsley, mommy does all of this for you two. I want to show you in every way what it looks like to chase your dreams with all you have, work hard to achieve your goals, and make an impact on this world. I love you two with all my heart and thank you for understanding the long nights, early mornings, travel, and grind that goes into making this happen. I hope that I make you proud.

To my bonus babies: Chelsea, Zackery Jr., Zavian, Zarian, Chrissiana, and Zackeaus, know that you can do anything you put your mind to, and having you in my life has brought about another sense of purpose for me. Together, your father and I will create a legacy that will prepare you for the life you deserve.

To my family: Mother, sister, brother, and extended family, you are my greatest love. To me, it's all that really matters because without you all, I am nothing. Thank you for riding with me in the good times and the bad times. You love me unconditionally and let me know that no matter what I can depend on you.

Dad, I know you're not here in the physical, but I want you to know that I will always love you, and I forgive you. Our bond was unique, and even through it all. I am and will always be a daddy's girl at heart. You were the first to expose me to business, and it is because of you that I have been able to try and succeed in that area of my life. You will forever be in my heart.

To Rachel G. Woodson: When we started working together, I was a mess, a broken-hearted girl with so much unhealed trauma, but together, we made this thing called life make sense. I am forever grateful for all that you are and all that you do. You have been here since the inception of *Overcoming Her,* and I know that making the decision to include you in my life was only a part of God's Divine plan.

To Jasmine Womack and the P31 Publishing Team: I knew the book was necessary. I knew the book would be impactful. I knew the book was a part of what God is calling me to do, but I had no idea how to make it happen. With your support and guidance, this book is a reality. Thank you for everything. You living in your purpose allows me to live out mine. I am blessed to have you be a part of this journey.

Lastly, to everyone who has supported me in any way including friends, clients, and mentees, because of you, I get to wake up every day and live in my purpose in the calling God has for me. I am a firm believer that when you give and serve, you put yourself in a prime position to receive. Your support is only confirmation of that. My job is to give of myself and the gifts that God has given me in an attempt to impact you in some way. I hope this book blesses you and helps you too live the life you have always desired.

Forward

As an international relationship coach and mentor, I have been blessed to work with thousands of women. I run into women who remind me of myself, and Simone is one of them. I didn't start off as her mentor, I started off as her relationship coach, but now I am a fan. It was in our first session that I thought to myself, *this girl has no idea about what God has in store for her life.* I am not just saying that because we are both from the same area.

I look at purpose as a blessing, and when God gives you more purpose than what you know what to do with, it can be a struggle to see past the pain. I know she was hiring me to be her relationship coach, but I saw so much more in her story. We continued to work on relationship sessions, but I would throw small assignments her way. I wanted her to not only find her purpose(s), but also I wanted her to be unafraid to walk in it. The more we began to go through the healing process, the more I began to encourage her. I asked her like I do most of my clients to trust me. We began to peel away the layers of her purpose. When you have so much that you can use from your pain to help others, you don't know where to start. As months turned into years, we developed a sisterhood as well.

It was no longer about the payments with Simone. I needed her to be great because God had shown so many great things that He had in store for her. I refused to let her give up on her purpose, and she kept trusting me and kept going. The Simone that you are going to read about is a story of you, your mom, your sister, your cousin, your friend, or your coworkers. Her life has so many layers of purpose to which people can relate, and those layers make people want to follow her footsteps. She will be an everyday Shero and an inspiration to so many women all over the world. What I love about her is that she never focused on how much money she could make because she was walking in her purpose. She was more worried about living and being a healed mother for her boys so she could be an amazing wife and give her boys the family they deserve. When it came to helping others, she was eager to help other women overcome their pain.

~ Rachel G. Woodson
International Relationship & Life Coach

Refusing To Quit Introduction

I remember being a 16-year-old girl who was unsure of myself and my future. I remember being in my junior year of high school and finding out that I was pregnant. I was a very active student in my high school. I was a part of every club and even was the captain of the cheerleading squad. I didn't know how this would fit into the life that I envisioned for myself. I was afraid, and I was unsure. I didn't know what I was going to do, but I knew the only thing that I could do was figure out how to continue to move forward.

I've often thought about life as being this destination to which you arrive. I think of life as a place of ultimate happiness; once you have career success, a husband, the degrees, the home, and the car, you are supposed to have a level of happiness. In my mind, you are supposed to feel a sense of fulfillment and have an idea of exactly who you are. Once you get there, it should be enough. I felt that once I got to that place that I always aspired to reach so desperately, I would have achieved my goal. However, no matter how hard I tried, it seemed like I just could never make it there. For me, life has always been about pushing through the challenges and obstacles and figuring out how to face the disappointment.

Even though I had a child at 16, I still managed to go off to college, graduate cum laude with a bachelor's degree in marketing, and start a business. I thought I was living the life that I was supposed to live. I was engaged to somebody who I met in the church. On the surface, it appeared that I had everything I could possibly want that would make me feel fulfilled, but there was still something missing. Then, the relationship failed. The bottom fell out, and I began the quest of trying to figure out my identity.

Throughout the journey of the last 32 years of my life, I've come to learn that no matter what cards life deals you and challenges in which you find yourself, as long as you don't give up on yourself, you always have another day to make it better. You have another opportunity to go after those goals. Chase down those dreams. Figure out whatever is happening in the in-between that you want to be different.

Life is definitely not about the destination. There's no place that I believe that you can ever reach that provides 100% fulfillment because life is full of peaks and valleys, ups and downs, and obstacles to overcome. The reality is that you have everything inside of you that you need to move forward towards the life that God has for you and towards the purpose for which you were created.

In this book, *Refusing to Quit*, the principles that I will share are truly things that I've learned throughout my journey through life. It's been a rough road. I have learned some hard lessons and had some tough experiences, but I wouldn't change my experiences for the world. All of those things ultimately didn't do anything but craft me, mold me, and prepare me for this very moment.

As you read this, if you're the person who is struggling to figure out how life all comes together, why things happen the way that they do, and what is the purpose that they serve, my goal is to encourage you. I hope my testimony empowers you. This book will provide you with real tools, resources, and key principles that you can apply in your daily life that will move you closer to that inner peace.

Experiencing peace does not mean that your life will be void of conflict. Peace is neither obstacle-free nor a guarantee that you will experience 100% contentment. Peace is the opportunity to understand that life is only 10% of what happens to you and 90% how you react to it. Therefore, let's get directly into it.

Key Principle # 1

Acknowledge the Pain

One of the biggest things that I had to understand in life and where I start at chapter one is dealing with your past. All of us have a past. We all have things to which we have been exposed to such as hurts, frustrations, childhood issues, abandonment issues; these things have molded us, crafted us, shaped us and our thinking, and made us who we are today. The reality is those very things become your compass through life. Depending upon what those lessons were or what those past experiences were, you've learned to cope; you've learned to just deal with life in the best way that you can.

For me, life was all about just trying to figure out how to cope before I truly took some time to deal with myself and work on my issues. My coping mechanism and the way that I lived life was through trial and error. I tried everything. I am somewhat of a risk taker. I consider it my gift and my curse because if it did not work, I would go back and try again. When I finally realized it wasn't going to work out or turn out the way that I thought it should, I would just avoid it. I was just trying to shift through whatever it was that was presenting the pain. I never stopped to really deal with the issues of my past. It took many years into my late 20s for me to want to take the time to acknowledge the pain that I was dealing with.

It takes a very strong person to address your own flawed thinking and the behaviors that you've developed over the years. This flawed thinking makes it extremely easy for you to have unhealthy habits and patterns. The errors in your logic provide justification for the circumstances that are taking place in your life.

I had to take some time to really understand where that emotion originated, what caused those behaviors, and what developed the insecurities, and I realized it all stemmed from me being the 12-year-old girl whose father walked away and did not take the time to be present in my life. His drug addiction was more important than being there for his children. I would often lead with the thought that I wasn't good enough. If I was not good enough for my father to stay around, then I wouldn't be good enough for anybody to stay around. I remember so many days thinking that and having that little small thought still tucked away in the back of my head. For many years, I lived my life hoping to gain the approval of the people who were around me. I was hoping that somebody would stick. I did not realize that it was all self-sabotage because I hadn't taken the time to truly deal with those issues like the disappointment of my father not being there.

When it comes time to deal with your past, you have to acknowledge the pain. That is key principle number one. When you are on this journey towards life and get where you desire to go, you have to acknowledge the pain. I was hurt. I was disappointed. I was bleeding emotionally on the inside, and subconsciously, I kept taking the same test over and over and over in life and failing because I made so many decisions out of my emotions. I was not taking the time to focus on the logic. I was not looking at situations at face value as far as what the reality actually was. I was truly making decisions from a dangerous place because my emotions changed very quickly. If you are a woman, or if you're anything like me, God designed us to be very emotional people. Making the bulk of my very important decisions out of my emotions only left me disappointed, frustrated, and hurt in the end.

Acknowledging the pain was the start of my healing process. Once I truly accepted the fact that I was hurting, it was time to identify who was responsible for the pain that I was continuing to feel. I had to identify the very first time in my life that I dealt with disappointment, hurt, or negative thoughts that left me feeling alone or abandoned and pinpoint its origin. Even though I was a child, and there were some things that were out of my control, which meant that I didn't have a big say-so in the outcome, I still carried around that baggage for 30 years of my life. For 30 years, I carried around things that I ultimately could not control. My subconscious actions and behaviors were only leading to more hurt and pain and were partially responsible for the vicious cycle that was happening in my life. This cycle was ultimately producing more dysfunction.

I stated how all of my decisions came out of my emotions and insecurities. I had a drug addicted father, and I watched him abuse drugs most of my childhood until finally my mom decided that she had seen enough and walked away. As the oldest of three siblings, I had the burden of being the support system for my mother. A large part of my childhood and my upbringing consisted of being the strong one. This responsibility at an early age included having my son at the age of 16, which was due to the fact that I had many insecurities that I had not dealt with. I was also in a five-year relationship that resulted in physical abuse and domestic disputes. I thought that I had found the thing that was supposed to be that happily ever after only to realize that when I should have been paying attention to the behaviors of the person, I was more concerned with not being alone. I was being deceived in relationship after relationship including friendships and romantic relationships. Married men claimed that they were divorced only to find out years and months later that they were lying. Even more recently, I had another child outside of wedlock. All of these missteps were attempts to fill the voids that were happening in my life due to the lack of love I felt because of decisions that were outside of my control as a child.

When I finally got sick and tired of being sick and tired, and I made the choice to confront or address the very first moment when the disappointment showed up, I finally started to feel as though I actually could navigate things through life. I actually could figure this thing out because I went to the source of my pain which was the place that I didn't want to confront the issues, and I had a tough conversation.

You may hear from time to time people say girls ultimately end up with or marry somebody just like their father, right? He is the first example of what a man is supposed to be to you, how he's supposed to treat you, and what that's supposed to look like. For me, my father was very unemotionally available and spend hardly any time with me. For the most part, I remember him being asleep on the couch with the TV playing. That's probably the extent of my memories of him. He never came to a football game to watch me cheer. He never came to any programs at school. He did not do any of the things that should be a requirement or the responsibility of a father who takes an active approach or an active role in his daughter's life.

That emotional unavailability showed up in my life in so many ways because I didn't have the guide or the example that I needed. There was no person who was there to say, "Hey baby girl, this is what you should accept, and this is what you shouldn't accept." He was not there to tell me, "This is what love really looks like, and this is what care is, and this is what happens when somebody cherishes you." Because I didn't have any of that, I started to live life on the trial-and-error philosophy. I never really took the time to identify what I wanted, and I learned what I didn't want through the mistakes, disappointments, heartbreaks, and failed relationships after failed relationships.

I had to confront my source. Yep, I know that for some of you, identifying the place that is the source of the pain, dealing with the past, and identifying the place that has been painful mentally are already challenging enough. However, thinking about having to confront that source takes things to a whole new level. I challenge you that if you are truly trying to walk in your purpose and gain clarity and figure out why life has been one stumbling block after another, confront the source. You can understand the "why" in life. You will understand why things are the way they are, why things turned out the way that they did, and why you felt the way that you felt.

You get so many questions answered when you make the decision to confront the source, and for me, it started with having that tough conversation with my father. I needed to understand why he couldn't be the father who I needed him to be, why was he so unemotionally unavailable, and why, no matter how easy it appeared that life could have been, he chose a different outcome. I needed to understand that, and once I gained the strength to sit down and actually have that conversation with him, I learned something so valuable. The reality was that he was a very hurt child and had a tough upbringing. He suffered from an incident that occurred in his life for which he was ostracized, ridiculed, and made to feel inadequate as a child because of a pure mistake. Because of that, he didn't learn what love looks like. People can't operate past their own level of understanding no matter what the situation or circumstance is. Without someone taking the proper steps to go out and get help, he or she will be unable to operate past his or her own level of understanding. Therefore, because he was a hurt person, all he knew how to do was continue to hurt people.

In that conversation, I was able to forgive. I was able to start the process of healing, and I was able to understand that although I didn't have what I needed as a child, it wasn't because I wasn't enough. It was because he wasn't equipped with the tools, and he didn't take the time to go out and get them. That was the worst part.

Taking the time to confront the source sets you free. It starts to make the things that seem so big feel so small. Although the conversations are never easy, being able to deal with your past and confront the areas that caused the pain, allow you to spend more time in your life focused on where your future is headed.

There was also a moment that I finally decided to share my experience with domestic abuse. I remember making the decision in my mind to have a conversation with my ex with whom I was in an abusive relationship. I remember the very first time that the abuse started, and it always progressively got worse until I finally made the decision that I needed to leave. In that moment, I left with nothing but myself and my son, and I was just thankful to be alive. However, this person from my past and I continued to have to come in close contact with each other. We attended the same church. Because my relationship with God was important to me, I knew that I needed to be in church. I knew the benefits of deepening my relationship with Him, but I was so uncomfortable seeing my ex every single Sunday. I know it's easy to say *well why didn't you just go to a different church*. Yep, I tried that too, but my church home was my church home, and I wanted to continue my membership there. However, knowing that it was a possibility that I could run into this person from my past made me very uncomfortable. I remember a time sitting on the church pew just looking around to see if he was somewhere in the building. The minute that the benediction happened at the end of the service I would move as swiftly as I could to get in my car and try to get home as fast as I could. I knew that I couldn't continue like that. I knew that it was no way possible that I could maintain my own mental health and continue having this dysfunctional process in my life.

I made the decision that I was going to stop running and deal with it. I was going to share with my abuser what it was like to live through that. Whether or not he offered an apology, acknowledged it, or owned it, it wasn't about him in that moment because it was about me. I arranged the meeting, and we had a conversation. I shared the details of the night that my life changed forever and how that experience affected me. I did not know if I was going to make it out of there alive. I remember yelling at my then six-year-old son saying, "Run next door to the neighbor's house and tell them to call 911." I remember my ex screaming at my son who was standing there watching me get beat and telling him, "You better not go anywhere." I remember looking in my son's eyes at the level of fear on his face and his inability to move because he wasn't sure if he tried to run outside if the aggression would turn from me to him. I recalled those accounts. I shared the level of paranoia that it put me in. Even to this very day, I do not like to argue with people. I will not argue with somebody. It makes me extremely uncomfortable. I had to sit down, and I had to set myself free and acknowledge the pain, and I had to say, "Hey look, whenever I see you, it makes me a little unsure, and it makes me a little concerned. I want to know that at the end of the day if we have to coexist in the same space, my safety is not in jeopardy." Once I had that conversation, and he shared his thoughts, feelings, and emotions while acknowledging my pain, I was able to move forward. No longer did that person or the abuse hold me hostage. No longer was I only bound by what I had gone through. Interestingly enough, that very experience that set me free was the first area in my life that I started speaking about publicly. I'll get more into that a little bit later as we go along, but domestic abuse was real.

I was 22 years old when I made the decision to leave the relationship after five years, and I knew that it wasn't just about surviving the domestic abuse. It was about truly understanding how not only did that relationship affect me, but also it even served a purpose in the present moment.

The change ultimately starts with you. You have to take control over how you process, deal, and address the things of the past. If for whatever reason you are not able to confront the source because of death, distance, or something that's completely out of your control, you still have to figure out how to deal with it and address your pain. Until you do, it's going to be very difficult to break the unhealthy habits and the cycle in order to switch the trajectory of your life. That subconscious programming of that unhealed path will find ways to show up more than you know. Once you're able to confront it and truly process it and deal with it, the transparency can show up, and there's no more shame. There's no more disappointment. There's no more of you not feeling good enough and questioning why it happened to you. You've owned it, and you've dealt with it. You've addressed it, and now you're free to live life or make the steps towards the life that you want to live. In that transparency, it gives you the ability to be a testimony. Use your experience to help others and yourself because it's not just about them. It's also about you.

I've said this already. The forgiveness is not about the other party. It's about you. It's about your ability to move forward. There have been so many situations in my life that if I choose to not forgive the other person, hold on to anger, and not figure out how I could move forward, there is no telling where I would be.

I remember when I was in the very early stages of *Overcoming Her*, and God said to me, "I need you to be a witness. I need you to use your story and share it with others because it's going to help people." I was like, "Oh no, I can't do that Lord. I'm way too private for that. I can't let the world know what I've been through, what I've seen, and what I've had to deal with. How is that supposed to work?" Therefore, I ran from it for a really long time. Then, I finally fell flat on my butt in another failed relationship with a man who lied to me, manipulated me, and took advantage of my own internal insecurities until I finally said, "Okay God, I have tried this so many times my way, and my way it's just not working. So, I'm going to stop running from what you're asking me to do, and I'm just going to start doing it." I was so hurt by the failed relationship. I remember not being able to figure out how to get to what God was calling me to do because I was still upset at the disappointment from the relationship failing. I was upset at the steps that I had taken and the sacrifice that I had made to try to make this work only for it to fail. I couldn't realize the beauty in the other side. Finally, I had to make the choice to forgive this person for his lies and deceit and my disappointment in him. I had to let it go. I had to understand that it wasn't just a waste of my time, but it was the thing that had to happen to move me to where God was trying to get me. Without that negative experience, I would have still been running. I would have still been saying, "Oh, no." So, I had to fall flat on my face. I had to because without that, I would have continued to think that I had it figured out. I would have thought that I knew enough about myself, people, and things that I could do things on my own. I would have thought *God, I got this.* That experience changed my life, and it finally gave me the push that I needed.

Once I made the decision to forgive the person who so drastically violated my trust and did exactly what he said he wasn't going to do, I knew that for me to heal from all of the layers of mess that had then become my life, I needed to go out and get some help. I needed to take the time to work on myself. I had to identify the unhealthy habits that I had such as the thought processes that affected my decision-making. I had to put my whole self on pause and truly deal with that.

Key Principle #2

Invest in Yourself and Your Healing

Key principle number two from dealing with your pain is once you've acknowledged and confronted it, go and take the time and invest in yourself. Hire a professional, find a therapist, or identify a coach who is going to help you work through those unhealthy decisions that you've made.

To break the cycle in your life and get to the place you have never been, you are going to have to do things that you've never done. I know it may be uncomfortable, and it may be unfamiliar to hire somebody to talk to so that you can work through issues and problems. However, when I tell you it can be the catalyst for the beginning of you stepping into your own, it's definitely worth it to do. It's definitely worth taking the time to invest in your own mental, emotional, and physical health.

After I ended the negative relationship, I felt moved to be bold enough to do what God called me to do which was to share my story. Before I got to the place at which I was willing to share my story, I hired the coach. I spent nine months working with her day in and day out, week in and week out. We had difficult conversations and talked about things that I had suppressed so far back into my mind that I almost thought I forgot about them. I did that until I knew that for me to really handle the magnitude of what was about to happen in my life, I had to deal with all of that stuff. It was so beneficial and necessary. It not only changed the way I thought about myself, but also it shifted the way that I thought about others.

When dealing with your past, some things you cannot do all on your own. If you had all the answers, it would have been already figured out. You would already know what exactly it was that you needed to be doing to get to the place that you desire to reach. There would be no need for you to read this book to be very honest with you. However, if you have this book in your hand right now, and you're desiring help to identify how to overcome the obstacles in your life, make the choice to invest in yourself and go out and get some help. Coaching and therapy are necessary.

Making the choice to hire a professional was by far one of the best decisions I could have ever made. It helped me get into alignment. Together, my coach and I developed a level of trust. With her, I gained the confidence to be transparent, own all the choices I had made in life, and recognize that through it all, there was something beautiful that would come out on the other side. We put together a vision that I had for my life, and I shared with her all the things that I desired to have. As I reflect on all of the things I have in my life that we discussed during our coaching sessions, I am so thankful that I made the decision to get some help navigating my obstacles.

Key Principle #3

Understanding Your Value

As you continue on this journey of navigating life's obstacles and challenges, two of the most important things that you have to constantly remind yourself of your value and your self-worth. This is key principle number three. Understanding Your Value. If you take moments to really truly understand who you are and whose you are as a child of the King, there's nothing that life can present to you and no obstacle that you can come up against that will prevent you from being able to move forward and achieve the things out of life that you really want to accomplish. As you understand your value, there are definitely some things that I think play a very important role in this process, and one of them is mindset mastery or mastering your mind.

Everything starts with a thought. Thoughts lead to feelings, feelings turn into actions, and actions create habits. If, ultimately, you want to see any change in your life, you have to sit back and think about the thoughts that were a part of the beginning of the actions that turned into your routines or your habits. If you can replace those bad habits, get rid of the negative thoughts, and keep yourself full of positive mentally stimulating information, then guess what? You've cracked the code. You figured it out, and you've managed to identify the ways to master your mind.

I remember in very low moments of my life and in moments during which I was not sure how things were going to turn out or if I would even be okay, I would often have these negative thoughts enter my mind. Sometimes, I would think *Oh my god, Simone, you're never going to make it, Do that or you're never going to get that job*, or *You're never going to make enough money to be able to provide for yourself and your son*. I remember many days being unsure of who I was. Until I realized it was very essential for me to control the way I was thinking about myself, I would feel hopeless, lost, and confused. Finally, I said *you know what. If I'm going to expect anything different out of life, I need to be willing to do something different,* and that meant changing the way that I was thinking. What was I actually listening to? What was reinforcing the thoughts that I was having? I decided that I needed to make a shift. For me, that shift was as simple as replacing the gossip on the morning radio show that I listened to on my way to work with Bishop T.D. Jakes on YouTube. His sermons always tended to be right on time for me, and they always spoke to exactly what I was dealing with at the moment. It didn't matter what I was dealing with, and I would often listen to those messages first thing in the morning. I would walk into my office as I was preparing for my day at work listening to his messages, and oftentimes, I would listen to his sermons all the way up and through my lunch break. His words encouraged me, uplifted me, and gave me hope. His sermons removed a lot of wasted time and energy that I spent listening and feeding my soul with things that didn't uplift me. It provided me so much clarity and peace. It allowed me to deepen my relationship with God, and it allowed me to start my morning off in the right place and with the proper mindset.

In mastering your mind, you have to be very aware of the messaging including the messages that you feed yourself on a regular basis. You have to be very aware of what you're listening to and watching and what you're scrolling through on a day-to-day basis because all of those things start to produce an emotional response. If you're not careful, those emotions can be negative. Before you know it, you've developed a very unhealthy habit.

Speaking life into yourself is also extremely important in mastering your mindset and your attitude. I know it's very common, and we may hear it a lot about affirmations, but when I tell you when you give words life, you verbally speak them into existence. You make them real when you proclaim them out loud. There's a certain energy that goes out with giving words life. Making it a part of your day to speak something positive into your life also plants good seeds. It plants the type of seeds that we want to ultimately have flourish in our lives. These seeds are that we want to be able to see sprout up, grow, and blossom. It's necessary if you're truly in a situation in which you are dealing with something that is considered a valley or struggle, and for whatever reason, it seems like you can't see your way through the darkness. Choose to speak life into yourself and into your situation, and your words will start to create a shift in the universe and in your atmosphere.

I want to share this experiment that I was reading about. I've always been a seeker of knowledge. I'm always a person reading and trying to advance myself from an intellectual perspective, and when I started to get serious about changing my mindset in my mentality, I would go out and research things that I knew that if I actually implemented, they would benefit me. I came across Dr. Emoto's Water Experiment. Dr. Emoto was a professor at a university, and one semester he had his class perform an experiment surrounding water. The whole classroom yelled negative, hateful words. They just screamed these words into the atmosphere. During that time, he froze the water as they screamed the negative words and then took the molecules of water and placed them under a microscope. He did the same thing with positive words. He had the class yell at the glass of water positive, uplifting words. He froze that water and then looked at the crystallization of the water in those two separate entities under a microscope. It was amazing what he found. When the negative words were being yelled and frozen into the water molecules, all of the crystals made these very ugly and nasty cracks and breaks. Then, the glass of water that was frozen during all of the positive words was very beautiful. The water made these nice harmonious curlicues and spirals in bursts almost as fireworks were frozen into the water. The positive and negative words produced two completely different outcomes. Dr. Emoto's Water Experiment showed me that words have power.

There is so much power in what you say out of your mouth which is why you have to always be aware and cautious of what it is that you are speaking aloud because it could be the difference maker between whatever circumstance you're in turning out in the best way it possibly could or in the worst way that it possibly could. Our bodies are made up of 60% water. If the water in the cup crystallized differently between negative words or positive words, and our bodies are made up of 60% water, what do you think happens to you if you are not speaking life into who you are? What do you think is happening on the inside of your body?

Developing healthy habits is critical and important to the steps that you take to begin and end your day. When you first open up your eyes in the morning, what is your daily routine? Oftentimes, we get so caught up in the hustle and bustle of life that we usually don't sit and take time to think about our day-to-day actions. We're kind of like moving on autopilot. We're kind of just shifting through life from one moment to the next and never really stopping to think about the habits that we're developing. We do not take the time to think about the reasons that we're doing what we're doing and why it is that life looks the way that it does. What I will tell you is that the way you start and finish your day is the difference maker between how you rest during your sleep and start off your day the following morning. When I wake up in the morning, the first thing that I do is not to reach for my phone. I don't make my phone my go-to option the first thing in the morning. For me, it's more about mental clarity and ,focus. For the first 30 minutes of my morning, I do not grab my cell phone. I don't pick it up. I'm not in a rush to check an email, respond to a text message, or check social media. I spend those first 30 minutes of my morning praying, meditating, and thinking through my day including all the tasks that I have to achieve. I also like to give thanks to God for allowing me to see a new day. All of those things are important steps in how I begin whatever task I'm seeking to complete. I want to say to you pay attention if you feel like you wake up in the morning with a certain level of anxiousness, and you feel like the hustle and bustle begins the moment you open your eyes. I challenge you to sit back and think about your morning routine and consider changing it. If that means waking up 20 minutes earlier so you can have a calmness to your day, it's worth it. If that extra 20 minutes will allow you to spend time meditating on who you are and what you hope to achieve, it's so worth it. It's so worth giving up a few more minutes of sleep to be able to complete or prepare for your day successfully.

That same process can be used for your night routine. One hour before bedtime, I do not pick up my phone. That's my complete unwinding time. That's when I reflect. I may watch TV, or I may not. It's my opportunity to relax. Oftentimes, I'm spending time with my young son. The last thing that I'm on is the phone. I try to ensure that I get all the things done that I need to get done prior to getting into the bed because once I'm in bed, there are no distractions. I don't want to go to sleep thinking about who did what, why they did it, and what the outcome is going to be. I don't want to go to sleep thinking like that. I want to go to sleep thinking about what I was able to achieve and what is it that I would like to achieve the following day. I want to thank God for seeing me through another day and move on from there.

Maintaining a healthy mindset is a continuous process. It is not true that if you do something one time, now you got it all figured out and don't have to do anything anymore. That mindset is the complete opposite of the truth. We are always and forever will be works in process. We will always try to advance or better ourselves, deepen our level of understanding, and push forward to the next place. Maintaining a healthy mindset is a forever process. You have to understand that it is not a destination that you're seeking to reach. It is just a journey. It makes life a lot easier to understand. For me, negative thoughts still show up from time to time no matter how much coaching and personal development I receive. I'm still human too.

There are moments in which I have doubts and negative thoughts. The goal though is to not stay stuck in those negative thoughts. I do not allow those negative thoughts to hold me hostage and keep me from being able to move forward or to move past them. I have developed a process of replacing negative thoughts with positive ones. Whenever I have a negative thought or start to feel like life is not going the way that I desire for it to go no matter if that's in business or with my children, I have developed the process of replacing my negative thoughts with the positive ones. One of the areas in which I struggled the most with the negative thoughts was my feelings about myself in regards to my relationship with men. I may have mentioned this already, but my father was not a very active father in my upbringing. He was present in the household until I was about the age of 12, but that's about all. He was physically there. Emotionally, he was not present, and then after the age of 12, not only was he not physically present, but also he was not emotionally present. My father struggled with drug addiction, and this made it very difficult for us to have any type of relationship. I often thought that his drug addiction was more important than anything else in his life because I saw the lengths to which he would go to supply his habit. I saw the things that he took out of the house to pawn, and he would leave my mother, my other two siblings, and me stranded to satisfy his habit. Finally, he left, and my mom said, "Enough is enough!" She said, "We're leaving this situation." I started to carry around the weight of feeling like I was not good enough for my father to stay around. I wasn't good enough to combat his addiction. I wasn't worth enough to him to want to be a part of my life. Why would I be worth enough to any other man to want to stay around? I literally would think that days upon days upon days. I had the negative talk on repeat in my mind. Oftentimes, the moment that a relationship would fail, I would say, "See, there he is again! Nobody's going to stay around. I'm not good enough to be loved. My father didn't even stay around." Subconsciously, because I believed that, that's exactly what I brought into my life. I attracted people who had no intention of staying around.

I've developed a process of replacing any negative thought with a positive one the moment that it enters my mind. The moment that I am consciously aware that I am thinking a negative thought, I cast it down and remove it, and I replace it with a positive thought. Now that we've talked about confronting your past, addressing the person who was responsible for the pain and heartache, and identifying some ways to master your mindset, it's time to focus on your future.

Key Principle # 4

Focus on the Positive

Controlling your thoughts means that you have to give yourself something positive to focus on. Put your brain power to use in the most productive way. Instead of spending the time, energy, and effort on the things that have hurt you or disappointed you, now we're going to completely focus on our future. As long as you wake up the next day with air in your body, you have another opportunity to make things better and push forward to get one step closer to the things that you truly desire. I don't care what that may be. Whatever it is, you have another opportunity.

One of the most recent things that I have had to struggle with the most is navigating the relationship with my youngest son's father. At the start of the relationship, we had big plans, hopes, and dreams of marriage. Yes, I'm not perfect. There was a pregnancy before the talk about marriage, houses, and careers. I thought he was going to be a part of my future. Very quickly into the relationship, I started to realize that what I had desired or planned was not happening and wasn't going to happen. Was I disappointed? Yes. Was I heartbroken? Yes. Was

I confused? Absolutely. I could not understand how a sudden shift or change took this whole life that we had planned together, and it all dissipated almost in the blink of an eye. It was a very mentally draining time in my life.

There were moments I wanted to give up, and I cried a lot of nights. I'm not the person who is omitted from the struggle and from the hard moments. Now, I just know how to deal with them better. Once I was able to process the reality of what was happening in my life, I made the decision that it was in the best interests of my two sons and me that we move forward. We moved forward in every way emotionally and physically. We stopped coexisting together inside of the same space, and I moved into my own home. I stopped thinking about everything that was going wrong at that moment in time and what my future was going to look like, and I started focusing on the things that I had the ability to control or determine the outcome. I thought more about the work that I was going to put in and the seeds that I was going to plant that were going to bear good fruit. It was important for me to not spend time focusing on what was or what wasn't, but instead, I wanted to think about my future and all that God still had for me. As you start to develop healthy habits and continue to navigate mastering your mindset, I will say even in those moments when the difficult times show up, or those old thoughts start to creep in, just take a moment and think about your future. Think about how bright your future is and what there is for you. Focus on what God has in store for your life.

I have personally adopted the philosophy of using gratitude to counteract any negative thoughts or feelings. It is impossible to be negative and thankful at the same time. You can't feel defeated by your current situation and give to someone who is less fortunate than you simultaneously. I challenge you to try this concept, whenever you feel the negative thoughts trying to creep in. Find someone or something you can give to or be grateful for, and watch the instant shift in your mindset. This is a great tool you can use to continually focus on the positive.

Key Principle #5

Identify Your Gifts

Do you know the difference between a gift and a talent? When we think about some of the most influential people in our lives whether they are celebrities, singers, painters, authors, preachers, teachers, their gift is the thing that has allowed them to reach or achieve that place in their lives that causes you to look to them for influence. It is important to know the difference. It's important to be able to understand what a gift is and what a talent is. I'm going to give you the Webster's dictionary definition of the two because I believe that is super important for us to know exactly what they mean. A "gift" is defined by Webster as "A present or anything that is given or bestowed." The word "anything" is defined as "The property of which is voluntarily transferred by one person to another without compensation." In other words, you didn't have to pay for it; it was given to you completely. A talent is defined by Webster's dictionary as "A special often athletic, creative or artistic aptitude. A person of talent or a group of persons of talent in a field or an activity." Now, I don't know how they define the word with the word, but Webster's Dictionary actually did.

In addition to that definition, they provided an additional statement which called a talent "a natural endowment of a person|".

I want to take it a step farther. If gifts we don't have to pay or ask for are just given to us and granted to us by God, and a talent is something that is a special skill or ability that you have, what separates the two? Well, here it is. Talents have to be perfected. You go out and get some type of extra training or additional development. You do something with your talent that makes it a little bit better. A gift, even though it's completely God-given, is something that happens naturally. It's something that you don't even have to work at, and you automatically are able to do it well. So, although I know the line is very fine between a gift and a talent, if you think about it that way, you should start to be able to clearly identify what your gifts are and what you're talented at because there's definitely a difference.

God gives us all gifts. Every single one of us has a special gift; our gift is something that nobody else can do quite like us. The one thing that makes you unique in this world of billions and billions of people is your gift. Beyond the shadow of a doubt, my gift is the ability to speak well. I've been speaking in front of large crowds of people and standing in front of churches, organizations, and classrooms for as long as I can remember. I remember being 9 years old in my childhood church and having to stand up and do the Welcome Program for the Children's Day or Youth Day celebration. I remember being nervous and not quite sure of myself but still being able to command the room and hold the attention of everybody who was there. After successfully doing that one time, it seemed like I was always asked to speak. Whenever my church would visit another church, I can guarantee that I was on the program to speak. Annually, my church would compete at the National Baptist Convention of America, and I was on the competition team. From there, it transformed into speaking in the classroom for presentation day to speaking in front of large groups of people. I did presentations and spoke to women as I empowered them on their journey. Nobody had to teach me how to craft out a message. I never went to any type of special training for that. I never ever took a college course around it. It was natural. It was something about my ability to be able to stand up in a room and convey information in a way in which people were completely engaged. It's my gift. I do it well, and it comes so easily to me.

Now, on the talent side, there are some things at which I consider myself to be pretty talented. I'm a well-rounded person to be very honest with you, and one of my other talents is my understanding of the ins and outs of the field of business. I remember starting my very first business at the age of 21. I was an undergraduate at the time at Texas Southern University where I was studying business with a concentration in marketing, and by my junior year, I felt like I knew everything that I needed to know to go out into this world and start my own business, and that's what I did. I dropped out of school, started the business, and started trucking down this journey of being self-employed. Being self-employed came with so many peaks and tons of valleys. There were moments during which it was really great and other moments when it was really tough, but that experience for me was life-changing. It was my first hands-on introduction into business. Eventually, I went back to school, completed my undergraduate degree, and earned a master's degree in international business, so business was my thing. My gift was speaking. My talents were my education and my ability to understand what works and does not work in the field of business. I'm constantly perfecting my talent and going back to educate myself in other conventional and non-conventional ways. I'm constantly reading books, listening to podcasts, or reading newspaper articles. Therefore, my understanding for business it's something that has been developed because of my commitment to it.

Identify your gifts that God has given you and figure out how you can use those gifts to fuel your purpose. Your gifts will always make room for you…always. No matter what that gift is, if God gave it to you, it's going to make room in your life. When I first started *Overcoming Her*, I had no idea what I was doing. I didn't understand back end systems and social media algorithms. I didn't understand website development or graphic design. I knew nothing of those things. I had no idea how to make them work, but the one thing that I did know without a doubt was that God asked me to share. In the very beginning, the only thing that I had or that I knew to do was to hire somebody to make a website for me, set up a couple social media pages, and then just start sharing. That's all I had; that's all I knew to do. All of the email marketing, sales funnels, and other things that I needed to know were completely foreign to me. I knew nothing about what it would take to develop a personal brand. I often said that I'm a private person. I have no desire to share my life with the world. I remember prior to founding *Overcoming Her* and developing this personal brand, months would go by before I would make a single post on social media. I prefer to live my life in the moment than try to capture the moment.

It was a challenge for me in the beginning to understand how my gift of speaking was going to serve me and the assignment that God had given me with *Overcoming Her*. I was overthinking it for a really long time, and that overthinking and my perfectionist ways slowed me down and kept me from moving forward or moving at the pace at which I should have moved. When I got back to the root of what God was asking of me, it started to make sense. Essentially, all He was asking me to do was use my voice to speak. He wasn't asking me to have it all figured out in the beginning, and He wasn't asking me to figure out how to turn sharing His grace and mercy into a business. That wasn't what the assignment was. The assignment was just to share. Once I finally surrendered to that and just started sharing, all of the parts in the business started to come together.

I remember my first time speaking publicly for *Overcoming Her* brand. I talked about my personal journey and my experience with being a survivor of domestic violence. One of my friends who has a large platform gave me my first opportunity to share with the world. I remember very vividly in the beginning being nervous and unsure how much I wanted to share, what I wanted to share, what I didn't want to share, and how it was going to all tie in together. After successfully standing strong and transparent and being a witness, there was a certain level of boldness and confidence that I developed. Then, it just became like the old days when Simone would stand up in front of a roomful of people, and she would deliver her welcome speech as a little girl. It's just like riding a bike. You never forget, and so it just took one time to get my bearings. Then, after sharing my journey with the Epic Fab Girl community, I started to receive opportunities to speak at large or small events in my local city. I started to create my own opportunities to just speak such as hosting webinars and live events. I became really bold about what it was that God asked me to do. When I start to feel like things are difficult today, and I'm not sure of the road that I'm on or if I'm doing this right, I go back to the root of what I heard God asked me to do which was share just as simply as I could make it. That aligned perfectly with the gift that He gave me.

Through all of it, I was able to identify and find my purpose. I was able to take all of the pain, the disappointment, the heartbreak from childhood from my father and failed relationships and low self-esteem issues, and use it to fuel my purpose. All of the pain that I experienced and the things that kept me bound up for so long ultimately worked together for my good. There was not one situation that I experienced that I couldn't use to teach, empower, or educate another woman.

Finding purpose and understanding of how to use your pain in your purpose is part of the puzzle. The other piece of it is figuring out how to walk in it and actually execute it. I truly believe that most people desire or aspire to identify their purpose in life. I hear it all the time. The women whom I coach and people with whom I have normal conversations are struggling and wanting to discover their purpose in life. Identifying your purpose is only the start of the journey. It's only the start of the process because now you have to be bold and walk in it. Now, there's a certain level of accountability that comes along with knowing what your purpose is in life. Oftentimes, you have to be willing to do it even if you are afraid, unsure, and uncertain of how things will turn out. You have to move forward. Purpose means that you move forward based on your faith, and your "why" has to be big enough to keep you going even when the path is unclear. Turning the obstacles that you have come up against into opportunities to make an impact on the world is the real game changer. My life came full circle, and walking in my purpose created opportunities for me that otherwise I would have never had.

In my very early stages of dealing with the trauma of my past and trying to understand why my life was going the way that it was going and why I was facing certain obstacles, I decided to go on a fast. This was May or June 2017. I was fasting, praying, and seeking God, and I was doing the devotionals. I had purchased the workbooks, and I was doing the Bible studies on my Bible app. I was seeking God with every ounce of my being because I was tired. I was tired of trying things my own way and not getting far in life. I was frustrated with having to completely start over and take tests repeatedly about God's will for my life. During this fast in 2017, God brought me right to Romans 8:28. The text states that "All things work together for the good of those that love God and are called according to his purpose." The text does not say that only some things work together for your good or only a few things work together for your good. The text says that all things work together for your good. Everything that I had to endure and overcome because I was seeking God with my whole heart and wanted to develop a relationship with Him was working together for my good. I mean I was in the middle of the Bible study during this fast, and I came directly to the description. I am no Bible scholar. I'm not the person who is going to be quoting new scriptures off the back of my head. Every time somebody says something, I don't have a Bible verse or a Bible lesson to teach you. I'm truly a work in process as far as reciting or knowing the Bible. This particular scripture spoke so much volume to me that I started to hold it in my heart. When I found this scripture, it all made sense. It all came together, and from there it was the name of the organization.

That scripture helped me come up with the name, *Overcoming Her*. I kept saying, "Man, what is it about me that I know will connect with people and that they will be able to relate to, understand, and grasp. What characteristic about me is it?" Overcoming obstacles is what came to me. No matter how the obstacle looked, I managed to overcome it. Between the counselor that I was working with at the time and me, we came up with the name, *Overcoming Her*. It's been life-changing because the reality was that for so many years, I was in my own way; my flawed thinking, negative self-talk, and my inability to heal from my past trauma and pain were my stumbling blocks. I was in my own way. Not only did I have to overcome the obstacles, but also I had to overcome myself, so *Overcoming Her* was the perfect name that described everything about who I was and what this business and brand was going to be all about. Then, God revealed the number 8 in Romans 8 and 28 and the Biblical definition of the number 8. It is significant because it symbolizes a new order or a new creation.

Overcoming Her was my rebirth and resurrection. The old me was gone, and I was now this new creature. The number 8 became very significant to me as well. You will see that consistently throughout my brand materials and merchandise because everything has a purpose. Everything is very personal to my own journey and to what I know God has called me to do.

Purpose is where you will find your peace. If you are that person who knows that there is something more for you, you often have that nudging feeling of unrest in your spirit. Your day-to-day life leaves you feeling unfulfilled, and you know that there's more out there for you. It is not until you identify your purpose that you will find the level of peace that nobody can understand.

We'll go into more detail in the future chapters about peace and what that looks like, but just know that everything you need to live in your purpose is already inside of you...everything. God gave it to you; it's there. Sometimes, we may need help trying to figure out how to bring it out of us but trust that it's already there. Your chance to turn your obstacles and life experiences into opportunities is waiting for you. Start taking action, become intentional about your decisions, and align yourself with the right people. You need a plan.

Key Principle #6

Have a Plan of Action

You need to understand the significance of having a plan and not just a plan that you've written down on paper or thought about. It needs to bet an actual plan of execution. What is it going to take you to go from point A to point B and then from point B to Point C? That can be a 6-month plan, a 12-month plan, a 1-year plan, a 3-year plan, or a 5-year plan. Having a plan gives you a framework in which you should be operating. It gives you the roadmap, and I mean a plan that you can truly execute.

I'm naturally a planner. I've always been a planner even as a small girl. As a young girl, I had my whole life planned out. I knew what I wanted to study in school. I knew what kind of grades I needed to get. I knew what kind of time I needed to dedicate to my studies. I planned out my days. I planned out my years, and that has carried on with me even into adulthood. Some things went as planned and others not so much, but that didn't mean that I wasn't mentally prepared.

We know that there is always a possibility that our plans can change, and God is ultimately in control, but one thing that I can guarantee you is that my planning and preparation always put me in the best position to be prepared for whatever would come. I was constantly strategizing and thinking of what the next goal would be or what the next task that I wanted to achieve. There were never any moments of complacency; there was never the feeling that I had arrived so I didn't have to do too much more. There has always been this innate nudging push in me to prepare myself to go after what I wanted and accomplish more of the things that I desired. I know that I would not have been able to achieve a lot of the things that I have been able to accomplish without proper planning. Once I have a plan in place, I take action.

One of my strongest suits that I know without a shadow of a doubt separates me from a lot of people in this world is my ability to move. Most people have really great ideas, gifts, and talents, and they just sit on them and don't do anything with them. They talk, dream, and think about their gifts, talents, and ideas, but they never move on them. Fear holds them back, or the uncertainty of what's to come keeps them stuck. One thing that I know for sure is that you will miss 100% of the shots that you do not take, so you have to take the shot you have.

I can openly say that every single thing that I have truly desired out of life and set out to do I've watched come to pass. Once the thought enters my mind, I accept it. I receive it in my heart, and I put together my plan mentally and then on paper. Then, I start to move in on it. Every single thing that I have truly set out to do I have achieved. Now, maybe it didn't go exactly the way that I envisioned it in my mind, and maybe there was a different lesson that I was supposed to learn throughout the course of the experience or the journey, but I achieved it.

I remember being 21 years old still in my junior year in college. I was studying business, and I thought I knew enough. I knew enough about what it took to start a business. I was hungry, and I was ambitious. I was ready to get out into the world and let the world know that I had arrived. With that ambition, there was also a big part of me that was very naive and green and thought that everybody thought the same way that I did. I innocently believed that everyone's intentions were pure. I believed that if I gave freely and honestly and if I was trustworthy to others, I should get that back in return. I learned very quickly in the world of business that's not the way that everybody operates.

My very first business was a durable medical equipment company. I remember sitting in a marketing class, and as we went around the room to do our semester introductions, I informed the class that not only was I in school full time, but also I also worked full time at a very large local cardiologist's office. Shortly after that class ended, I was approached by this gentleman saying, "Hey, you know I'm in the medical equipment business, and I think that you know some people that can be a great asset to my business. I would love to sit down and talk to you more in depth." Mind you, I'm an ambitious go-getter, so when somebody starts to talk to me about business and about networking and connections, that gets my blood pumping. I get excited, and I am eager for the conversation we're going to have. The gentleman proceeded to tell me how he just would like for me to do some marketing for him, and I said, "Oh, this isn't too hard. Let me learn the ins and outs of this business."

A year and a half down the road, I started to realize that the relationship was not mutually beneficial. He was doing a lot of the receiving, and I was just doing a lot of the giving. I made the decision to separate myself from this person and go into business for myself. I had spent enough time in his office and around his business that I felt like I knew what was happening. I jumped in headfirst. I said, "Hey, this isn't too hard. Everybody knows somebody who needs medical equipment." I started the process of setting up this business. Little did I know that I was stepping into a whole world of insurance billing, health insurance policies and procedures, and medical accreditation, and it was so overwhelming. By this point, financially, I was invested. I spent all of the little money I had saved. I even went out and took a loan to start the business, so now it had to work right. I was moving from a place of desperation, and that was not a good place from which I was making business decisions.

I was forced to go back to the same person who I felt was using me a year and a half previously because he introduced me to the business. I sat down with him, and I said, "Hey, look, I started my own company, but I'm lost now. I don't know what to do. I think I need a consultant. Can you come on and help me from the point that I'm at now?" Of course, he said yes, but he came at a very high price. He agreed, but under the conditions that he would receive 50% of the earnings of everything that he referred to the business. That was an extremely high price, It came at the price of my integrity, my freedom, and my better judgment. Ultimately, he took all the profits while I had all the liabilities that I didn't know about at the time, but I was desperate, so I moved forward only to find myself in a more difficult position sometime down the road. The decision to hire him as a business consult lead to him referring fraudulent business to me because he wanted quick money, and it resulted in me having to fight a federal indictment for 3 years. After years of dealing with U.S. prosecutors, lawyers, judges, courts, and co-defendants, I was exhausted and just wanted this all to be over, I was sentenced to 13 months in a federal prison camp in Bryan, TX, which for me at that time felt like an eternity. I had no idea how I was going to survive prison.

I was a young, naive, small town girl who was now having to face the reality of being away from my family and most importantly my son for 13 long months. I was terrified. I remember the day I surrendered to the prison. I was placed in solitary confinement because it was a Saturday, and I thought *I can just do the whole 13 months here so I won't have to interact with anyone.* That's just how scared and unsure I was. Surprisingly enough, I quickly met some really interesting women from all different backgrounds, and I was able to be a light for them in such a dark place. They saw me, and they saw hope. I walked and talked differently, and I was even inspiring them in their current situations. Because I had a college degree, I was able to become a GED instructor, and I helped several women obtain their certificate so that they would have more options upon release. In hindsight, being in prison for 13 months was not that hard. Today, I refer to it as a "vacation" because at moments, I had convinced myself I was just on an extended vacation. The hardest part was being away from my son. However, I am a true believer that God does not waste any experience that you have to go through. All experiences have a purpose.

Many nights, I laid in the prison bunk and thought *Oh my God, my life is over. I am never going to be able to find a job to support myself. I won't have any friends who will understand this, and no man is going to want to be with someone that has had to endure this. My life is over.* Many nights I thought about suicide, but everytime, my mind wanted to tell me to freak out, my spirit would tell me everything is going to be ok. Whenever I would get overwhelmed with negative thoughts, a very calming feeling would hit me. It's almost hard to explain because I couldn't freakout even though I wanted to so many times. I had this peace that was beyond my understanding at that time. Now, I understand why I consistently would have those calming feelings. It was because of purpose. From the time I returned home, everything in my life fell right into place. I didn't miss a beat. The people who were really supposed to be in my life were right there when I returned. I returned to school and completed a 2 year MBA program in International Business and Supply Chain Management. Getting a job was never a problem. I had no obstacles surrounding employment and before returning back to full time entrepreneurship, I was making a very nice salary at a real estate servicing company, and on my 33rd birthday, I married the man of my dreams, a man who loved me, flaws and all. All the things that I was so worried about seemed to not have any relevance. However, the biggest business lesson that

I always took with me from that experience was to understand the importance of doing your due diligence.

Let me remind you, I was only 23-years-old at the time of my federal indictment. I started the business at the age of 21, and in those 2 short years, I learned so much. Life felt like I was in a whirlwind because things changed so quickly. However, in those very early years in business, I learned the importance of planning and execution. I learned the importance of doing your due diligence, doing your research, knowing who you're dealing with, vetting people and checking out their background, and making sure that they are who they say they are. I learned very valuable lessons at that time that I wouldn't trade. A plan is nothing without execution.

Even now, as I sit here, and share with you my principles and the things that I've learned throughout my journey through life and how all of it has worked together for my good, *Overcoming Her* is just another example of how life's lessons all work together towards your life purpose when you make the decision to execute what can be achieved. Even after many years of trying to stray away from what God called me to do, finally, I said, "You know what, Simone. No more running and no more trying to do it your way. Just surrender to God's plan. Let's try it His way for once." It still took a certain level of planning and execution for that decision to manifest into what it is today.

Spend some time really identifying what your long-term plans are and what short-term steps you need to take to get you there. Visualize the things that you're working on. The keyword is "working", not just visualizing what you desire but what you're actually working on it. At the beginning of the year, everybody looks at the new year as a new opportunity to be this new you and to start all these amazing goals and projects. We throw vision board parties. We put together vision journals. We have all these things to get us hyped up about what happens at the beginning of the new year, but oftentimes, we fill that with things that are unrealistic. We go through the magazines, and we cut out the picture of the big fancy car, fancy house, or a big old diamond ring or the wedding dress. We do this even if we don't have a single prospect in sight and are not dating a single soul. We do it if we are not in a position to buy a $150,000 car or don't have $10,000 to take the vacation way across the world or Bora Bora. We cannot afford to go on an expensive vacation but we put the tiki huts on the vision board. If it's all in the sake of just fun, then that's great, but I see visualizing the things that you're working towards from a completely different perspective. I'd rather spend my time more productively, and I encourage you to spend your time visualizing things that you can actually apply to your life. Focus on things for which you actually have the available resources to move you closer to the goals that you set for yourself. Do not focus on the far-fetched ideas, dreams, and visions but focus on the real tangible stuff. The reality is if you take one step and then two and then three steps, eventually, you will reach the destination that you seek. The results show up. You just have to be willing to continue to take the steps, but the vision board, the vision journal, and the pictures that you have posted up around your house those should be realistic items that move you one step closer.

At the beginning of 2018, the whole vision board craze really was just booming. Everybody I knew was throwing a vision board party, and it was fun to go and spend the time and fellowship with other people that I enjoy being around, but I remember being very intentional about what I was placing on this vision board. While everybody else was kind of just doing it for the sake of doing it, I understood the significance of making a visual of the life that I desired to live and the things that I wanted to achieve in 2018. I want to just kind of share a few things with you from my board. One of the things at the very center of my board was the cover of this book, and underneath it I said, "Write the book." This was January 2018. It was one of the things that I knew that I needed to finish in 2018. I didn't finish the book in 2018, and I didn't get it published until much later in 2019. In February 2018, I found out I was pregnant with my youngest son, and life changed. The plan altered the vision change, but I want to show you that just because the plan changes does not mean that the goal or the destination is any different. The moment that I had the opportunity to pick back up with the vision that I had for my life, I got right back to it, and I executed on it. Once I realized that maybe I didn't have the ability to do it all by myself because there were parts of the process that I didn't understand, I went and found some people, and I got their assistance. I invested with them so that way they could then help me get to where it is that I needed it to be.

Another really big thing that was on that big vision board for 2018 was becoming a "full-time entrepreneur." That was one of the goals for 2018 that came to pass involuntarily. I desired to go back into full-time entrepreneurship, but because of my experiences at 21 and 22 and 23 when I was very ambitious and tried a bunch of stuff with some successes and failures, I knew the struggle of being a full-time entrepreneur. I knew the sacrifices that came along with that. I also understood the fluctuations in cash-flow. Although I desired it desperately because I knew that was where I would thrive, I knew that God was calling me to something greater than what my time would allow me to do while working a job and working my business part-time. I didn't know how it was going to happen, but with obedience and the decision to continue to take the steps forward, full-time entrepreneurship happened involuntarily.

The job that I thought that I was going to be on for several more years and planned my 30s around fired me, and I was three months pregnant. What was I supposed to do? Should I go out and secure another job as a soon-to-be mom or should I buckle down and figure out how to make my business work with my newly found freedom? Well, I chose option number two. I got serious about my business. I got serious about putting some foundational pieces in place, and my goal now is to stay a full-time entrepreneur for the rest of my life. Now, that's my plan. My desire is to never have to go back to work for anybody else. I'm doing the work; I have a plan, and I know what's required of me to make that happen. Remember, all goals and plans need to be SMART(Specific, Measurable, Achievable,

Relevant, and Time-bound). If you develop a goal and a plan that meets all five of these areas, I can guarantee you results will show up. If you can make a SMART goal and execute it, success will happen. However, there is no shortcut to complete the work. It has to be done. The type of actions that are required to move you forward and move you closer to your goals are going to cost you something.

My day to day looks like three tasks. If I can get three tasks done a day off my to-do list successfully from start to finish, I have had a successful day. If you can't manage 3 tasks, work on 1 task. One task a day that you can complete or finalize in totality that moves you one step closer to your goal is a win. Life is busy. Most of us have jobs, and some of us have husbands, kids, life responsibilities, church obligations, social organization, and friends. It is so easy to get distracted and leave things incomplete. Scheduling dedicated time to work on your purpose is necessary. Carving out those moments when you can give 100% of your attention, brainpower, and resources to your goals is necessary.

I was working full-time in a corporate job, and I would work on my business part-time in the evenings. I worked all day. I was up at 6:30 in the morning and would be in my office by 7:30, and most days, I was there until 6:00 at night. I would get off from work and come home and start mommy duties including preparing dinner, cleaning, making sure my son was done with his homework, and preparing him for bed. Once all of that was done, I would still have to turn on my brain and get to work for *Overcoming Hurt*. Once everything else in the house was done, I would sit at the computer, and I would study, read, and complete one of the tasks that was on my list. Some of the tasks required me to figure out how to create my own social graphics. I would educate myself on that. Most times, I would stay up until 2:00 to 3:00 in the morning. I still had to be back up at 6:30 the next morning to get ready for work to do it all over again. That was my life consistently for about five or six months while I was putting the foundational pieces together for my business, but my "why" was so big, and I was so committed to getting to the other side of life and getting out of my own way that I knew that I couldn't give up on myself. I couldn't give up on this because it was going to change not only who I was, but also it was going to change the lives of so many other people.

In December 2017, I remember God revealing to me that it was time for me to leave the job. In my opinion, I just became obedient to what He was asking me to do. He gave me this plan in 2015. I ran from it for two years. September 2017 was when I really started getting serious about *Overcoming Her* and trying to create something. October 2017 was the first time that I spoke publicly about anything that I had been through in life, and that's when I shared my journey with domestic violence. I was still putting a lot of the foundational pieces of *Overcoming Her* together, but the framework was there. God said in December 2017, "Hey, it›s time for you to leave this job." I was like, "Oh my. God. No. I have to pay rent, my car note, and I have a son I have to provide for. I can›t leave my job." *Overcoming Her* wasn't making any money, but my confirmation was so clear that it was time for me to go in December 2017, but I didn't move. I stayed there because I needed the paycheck.

In April 2018, I got fired, and I remember going into a moment of panic just for a split second. I said, "Oh my God, what am I going to do? I just lost my job?" Then a feeling of calmness came over me, and in that moment, I heard God's voice so clearly tell me, "But I told you to leave in December, and you didn't move at all. You stayed. So now, I had to take it away." That's exactly what happened, and I have not been back to work for anybody else since then. After losing that job, it freed up my time to be able to devote 100% of my attention to my purpose. All of the changes that had to come because of the change in my job situation were just adjustments because life is not a sprint. It is not a sprint to a destination. It is truly the journey. Every season brings about different experiences. Oftentimes, I would always think that life was just about arriving at this place right at this destination of complete happiness that I envisioned for my life. I'm finally starting to realize that each season births or brings about a different set of experiences, challenges, highs, and lows. It's all just about embracing the moments, learning as you go, and making the journey the best that it can be.

Key Principle # 7

Differences Between Success and Failure is Consistency

After being forced into full-time entrepreneurship in April 2018, I knew the only way that my business was going to grow and work was if I got consistent. Consistency was key. Results show up when you stay consistent. You have to show up every day for yourself, your business, your clients, your children, or whatever it is that is at the top of your priority list. Mastering the skill of consistency is truly the difference maker when you want to start to see change. Consistency is not always easy. It takes a certain level of discipline. Discipline is what's essential when you are trying to develop a level of consistency because the distractions are there. The distractions are going to always be there, and they're going to always show up. You have to figure out how to navigate life and continue to complete one task a day that moves you closer to your goals even in the moments when the distractions are there.

Never forget the value of investing in yourself. Understand the difference between a cost and an investment. Most people don't even know the difference because you associate it with spending money out of your account or out of your pocket. We tend to just think about it like that. Costs don't give you any return on what you spent. You don't get anything back. An investment, however, is an exchange. I give you money, and in exchange, I get something that I need to move forward. Don't ever sidestep the investment into yourself and into your business, your life or your relationships. That investment can be an education, it can be coaching, or maybe it is systems, tools, resources. Don't be afraid to spend the money. You can only get so far for free.

Like I stated earlier, when launching *Overcoming Her* was brand new for me, I knew nothing about operating online in a digital space using social platforms for business. All of my formal business training was done in the standard traditional model in a college classroom. I had to take some time and go and educate myself. I had to understand what was it going to look like to actually launch something and have it work. I spent countless hours taking advantage of all of the free tools that I could find. I took advantage of the free webinars, free eBooks, all of the free resources that were out there. Once I exhausted the information that was shared on the free side, I realized that I had to invest in myself and in my education. I signed up for a coaching program that cost me almost 5,000$ for 12 weeks. Depending upon what your perspectives are and the way your bank account is set up, 5,000$ could either be a whole lot of money or very little money. For me, at that moment in time, it was a significant investment, but I knew that I needed the education that was being offered, so I did it. I paid for the course. I paid for countless numbers of webinars and tons of eBooks and materials and continued my pursuit of education and mentoring opportunities . Continuing education does not stop. You have to continuously and consistently invest into yourself, your brand, your business, and your relationships.

You should never reach a point at which you feel like you have it figured out because if you do, that means your goal just isn't big enough. It's time for you to go back to the drawing board and create some new goals. We should always be evolving and pushing ourselves to reach and aspire for more. Put yourself in a position to be able to help and serve as many people as you can. One of my favorite personal finance gurus is Dave Ramsey, and his methodology states that once you have reached a level of personal success, you give it all away. He calls it his baby step number seven. I love this concept because it makes everything that you aspire to achieve in life all about you; it is truly about making an impact on the world.

Remember, it's going to cost you something. To whom much is given, much is required. That is one of the most powerful statements ever. Walking in your purpose is going to separate you from people, places, and things but choose that purpose and choose what God called you to do over anything. People may judge you, and most won't understand it but find your peace and know that you're living for something greater than just yourself. You're living for what God has called you to be. You have to truly understand what your "why" is, and that "why" has to be so big that it keeps you going even when you're frustrated, confused, or unsure. That why has to be a consistent prevalent factor. My why was all about obedience.

I had experienced life for so many years on my own terms and thought that I was smart enough to have it all figured out. Every time I fell flat on my butt, I would hit my head up against another brick wall. I would have one hurdle after another. Oftentimes, something just didn't go quite right; it was like I would almost get there. I was so close that I could taste it, but then BAM!, another obstacle. Even in my relationships with the opposite sex, I desired marriage, and it's like no matter how I did it, I could almost always get there but never achieved it. I was engaged 3 other times before meeting my husband. However, I am so thankful that none of those other relationships worked out. While I was in the midst of it, I couldn't understand what I was doing wrong.

In all of the prior business endeavors that I've had, I've always experienced some level of success. I never had quite enough success to push me over the threshold and to the level that I believed I was capable of achieving. My business goals have always been to be a multiple business owner and generate millions of dollars per year. Some of the things in my personal life that I shared earlier in the book that I thought that I dealt with in counseling have shown back up in my life to the point that I want to go back to the starting line. Some of these things that I was told I was healed from are still struggles for me such as my self-esteem. I was exhausted with life. That's where my "why" was. I've tried every way possible including my own way for 30 plus years. Now, it's time for me to try to do this God's way, and that's what I remind myself to do every single time that I start to overthink the process or get frustrated with results. When I don't feel like things are moving as fast as I would like for them to move or when opportunities aren't coming as quickly as they should or things aren't going the way that I believe that it should go, I constantly remind myself, "This is not your way, Simone; this is God's way." I step back and say "Guide me in the way that you want me to go. You make the way, Lord."

My fear of disobedience is so great that no matter what, I have to continue to move forward because I want to do what God is asking me to do. Disobeying what God asked me to do only results in more disappointments, frustrations, and heartbreak. At its simplest form, all God asked me to do was to share my life, story, and journey with the world, and it's going to reach hundreds of thousands of people. Be a witness to what it looks like when you don't give up on yourself, have faith, and move on the assignment. Your "why" needs to be that big if not bigger. As soon as you start to realize your "why" and walk in your purpose, there will be a level of separation that will happen. That level of separation will come before the elevation because everybody in your life is not designed to go with you to the level to which He is trying to take you. Everybody can't come. The person with whom you want to be in a relationship so badly is not equipped to go where God is trying to take you because he or she is not prepared. That person is going to be a weight that's holding you down, so you have to let it go. In the moment that you let that go, you'll be surprised by how clear things become because oftentimes, those people, places, and things that were holding you up are distractions and time robbers. They keep you so wound up in them that you have no time to spend in the presence of God. You have no time to spend hearing His voice and understanding what He's called you to do, and you definitely don't have any time to execute what He says. Therefore, you have to separate yourself from some of those people, places, and things, and that separation comes before the elevation.

I had a childhood friend for almost 15 years, and I remember right before getting serious about *Overcoming Her* in late 2017, I had to walk away from the friendship. This was somebody who was my best friend and somebody in whom confided about a whole bunch. She saw me in some of my darkest moments, and we traveled the world together. I thought she was going to be a part of my life forever and would be my maid of honor in my wedding and godmother to my children. That was the type of friendship that I thought that I had, but I also realized that she almost felt like a leech sucking the life from this relationship because it required so much of my time, energy, and effort. I was not being what this person needed me to be when she needed me to be there and that made me feel that the friendship was in jeopardy. At 16 years old, I've always had the love and support of my family. After having my son at 16 years old, my friend stepped right in, and my siblings also helped me. My best friend and I at 16 years old worked at the local grocery store as cashiers. Some days, we would work the same shifts, and there would be other days that we didn't. When we would get off from work around 10:30p.m. some nights, she wouldn't have a ride home from work, and I would get in my little car and leave my son with my mom or my sister to go pick up my friend from work because she didn't have anybody to come and get her. I did not want her to call a taxi because it would have cost upwards of $30, but I would show up time and time again because that was the nature of the friendship. There were moments when she would give back to me, but they were rare and often came with a lot of complaining.

One moment, I was going through a very difficult season in my life. I was in a relationship with somebody who had not been honest with me, and I found out the truth and that I was pregnant, and I needed to talk to my friend. She was out of the country on vacation, and I said, "Hey sis, the moment you get back in the States please call me. I really need to talk to you." This was a couple months before her birthday, and we were planning another trip to go to Dubai. I kind of told her a little bit of what was going on, but we couldn't talk too much in depth because she was out of the country. When she got back, I never heard from her. She never picked up the phone to call me and didn't check on me to say, "Hey, you good? What's going on?"

After two weeks, I knew she should be back from her vacation, and I started wondering what was going on, but at that point, I realized that she was purposely not picking up the phone to contact me because she was upset at the fact that my situation may prohibit me from going with her on her birthday trip to Dubai in a couple months. However, that was the farthest thing from the truth, but she had already formulated that opinion in her head, so instead of just being the good friend that I needed her to be right then in that moment, she chose to make it all about her. That moment was when I realized that the friendship had run its course. I recognized that our season had come to an end, and it was time for me to stop living to please her or somebody else. It was time for me to make the decisions that were going to put me in the best place and give me the most peace. Ultimately, I ended up having a miscarriage, but she wasn't there for that, and I had to navigate that with just the support of my family.

It was really heartbreaking because this was somebody with whom I had 15 years worth of a friendship. She had been there for some of my most difficult times, but it's amazing that as life goes on, you have to teach people how to treat you. Over the course of the years of friendship, we developed a type of understanding in which I kind of did all the compromising, and she was content with being the one who did a majority of the receiving. Making the decision to walk away from the friendship freed me up mentally, emotionally and time-wise to focus on my purpose with my business. If that friendship would have continued to thrive, I would have never had enough time to develop the things with *Overcoming Her*. We always had to be out at brunch, a day party, or at happy hour, and I would not have had time for other things that were important to me.

Separating myself from that friendship put me in a position to prosper, grow, and develop myself and my business so I could start to walk in my calling; it freed me up to do that. Don't be afraid to let things go and step into the new season of your life. God is going to send greater your way to replace whoever or whatever leaves your life. Don't hold on to people just for the sake of holding on to them. If the friendship, relationship, or partnership is not mutually beneficial to the point that both parties gain something from it, it's okay to let it go. Be comfortable with evolving in your personal growth, faith, and your journey. Change is a proponent to growth. Things grow and change, and you must be willing to allow change to come and flow in your life. You will grow, and your vision will change. The destination will stay the same, but the road that you take to get there may be different so be flexible, open, and aware and definitely don't allow the change to become a distraction.

Understand that once you make the decision to walk in your purpose, attacks and distractions will come. There is no sidestepping the difficult moments. You just have to understand that the role may look different, but the goal is still the same. The enemy knows your areas of weaknesses. He hears your prayers, and he knows what will tempt you, and as you start to move in your purpose, the goal is to keep you from that. He is going to tempt you and attack that very area. My weakest spot is my relationships. I desire and want them. I've made life decisions based on relationships so many times. I got pregnant with my youngest son in February 2018. I was unwed and unsure of my future. Because I desired the relationship and thought that I was on this path of purpose, I thought that everything that I was doing was moving me in the direction that God had for me. I made a decision based on what I thought I knew. I didn't go and see God for His confirmation at all. I said, "Oh well, since I'm doing what God asked me to do, this must be it." However, one thing that I know for sure is that everything has a proper order, and anytime things go outside of that order, they cannot still all work together for your good. God definitely has an order in which things should go, and you have to learn lessons from His process.. There's an order that life should follow. Because He also gives us the ability to have free will, oftentimes, we go outside of that order, but there definitely is an order that He expects us to follow.

After getting pregnant in February 2018, I was confused because it was unplanned, and I didn't know how it was going to fit into my message, purpose, and audience with *Overcoming Her*. I had no idea how that was going to work in my life, so I took a six-month hiatus. The book that was on my vision board for 2018 didn't get written for that very reason. I took a hiatus to regroup. I had to figure out what was the purpose. I had to get quiet and spend time with God and really truly understand how everything was still going to work together. There were still some things that I had planned for the year that didn't happen. One thing I know to be true is that when I get in my most vulnerable state with God, and I seek Him with my whole heart, all of my answers are always revealed, and that's what I had to do again in February 2018.

I received my confirmation from Him which was, "Simone, pick yourself back up, dust yourself back off, polish yourself up, and realize that your assignment hasn't changed. What I'm asking you to do hasn't changed. There's somebody else out there that's going to be able to understand and relate to you even more with your current position in life. You just continue to move forward." That's exactly what I did. Now I'm more disciplined and focused than ever. I'm aware of the attacks of the enemy, and I'm 100% knowledgeable he'll show up and hit the place that's the most vulnerable and the weakest. I don't ever let my guard down, and I stay connected to my source because He keeps me on the desired path that He has for me.

Key Principle # 8

Be Prepared

You have to know that to whom much is given, much is required. Are you prepared for the things that you are praying for? You will have to experience a level of separation before elevation, and evolution and change are necessary proponents to growth. This whole journey is going to evolve and change, and it will grow you in a lot of areas, but all of it will work together in perfect harmony as long as you continue to work.

After you've prepared yourself with the actions, and you're completing the task and getting the work done, you're ready to start manifesting the life that you are pushing towards every day. Before anything can show up in the physical realm, you have to believe that you're capable of achieving it. It all starts in the mind and your thoughts. If you can think it, you can achieve it. The thought came to you for a reason, and you have to be aware of that small voice. That small voice has to ring out very loudly when you get those instinctive thoughts.

I've always been told that I'm a really great speaker. I remember being in college and having to stand up and give presentations while all my other group members were scared. I was knocking the presentation out of the park. I never thought in a million years that I would be speaking publicly or that I would be coaching people and changing lives. Once I made the decision to be obedient to what God called me to do, I envisioned it all. I envisioned traveling around the world, speaking and coaching people, and helping them get to the place in life that they desire to go. I've mentally manifested this already. I can see it so clearly. Now, it's just a matter of me doing the work in the physical realm that's going to allow it to show up in the physical, and it's already happening. It's already moving. Things are already shifting, but it starts with the thought and envisioning the life that you want to live. You have to pay attention to the small details because they are key.

Most of the time, when somebody asks you, "What do you want out of life or what do you want out of your business?," the responses are often very vague and general. You say, "Oh, I want my business to be successful. I want to be able to retire at 45, 55 or 65." They are very general statements. When I say you have to envision the life that you want, I mean even to the very small details This key principle is what plays a big part in developing your plan and then taking the action. If you can get very specific about the vision that you have, navigating the road to get there becomes a lot simpler. For example, I have a vision for my life. I have envisioned writing three books, having opportunities to speak twice a month, developing a very corporate training style setting, and traveling all over the country and globally. I have it nailed down even to the price that I'm going to charge companies to use my services. I've mapped out how many lives I need to impact in my coaching and mentoring business to be able to scale it to the level I need to be successful. I have even narrowed down my focus to the number of people I want to reach. My plan is extremely detailed. It is not a vague, *oh I want to make $100,000 this year,* plan without specific details.

I knew at the time that I started to walk in my purpose, I did not want to live life through trial and error anymore. For many years, I had no clear direction, and everything for me was trial and error. I would try something, and when that something didn't work, I would say, "Okay, I can't do that anymore. Let me go and try something else." That was in my personal life, relationships, and business. Trial and error represents a hard way to live life. You will be beat up, bruised, emotionally broken, and mentally exhausted; it's a hard way to go through life. I decided to get off of that train and get very clear and specific about the vision that I had for my life including the steps that it would take for me to get there. I narrowed my focus to the tasks each day that I was going to have to manage to get me closer to that goal, the people with whom I needed to align myself, and the business investments that I needed for my business to aid me along the journey. Once I had that all figured out, I just had to believe it and receive it. I believe so strongly that nobody or nothing can come along and tell me anything different. There's nothing left for me to do but the work. There are no shortcuts to the work, but after implementing all of the principles that I've referenced throughout this book, the life that I have always desired that was once hard to envision is possible. You have to believe that without a shadow of a doubt, you deserve to live that life. You deserve to have that level of happiness, and every single thing that you've ever had to go through was just preparing you for the life that you desire. Step two is you have to commit to doing the work and figuring out whether it's going to be an extra hour in the morning or a few extra hours at night on your weekends; what are you willing to sacrifice to get the work done? Step three is to receive what you have been working towards and act as if it's already done.

I know in the very near future in less than five years, I am going to be standing on stage in front of tens of thousands of people educating, empowering, inspiring, and providing them with the tools to navigate their own lives. I know that nobody can tell me anything differently. I believe it, and I'm doing the work. I receive it, and I see this shift already starting to happen. I see people starting to show up who are in perfect alignment in my life. I see Divine connections being made, but you can't go to step three without being sure about step one. I had to believe it and then receive it.

Key Principle # 9

Define Your Own Success

As you arrive at the place of purpose, walk in it daily. When you put together plans and execute them, you will find yourself at the place you've always dreamt of. Live life on your own terms the way that you've always desired. A key principle that is so important for you to remember is that you get to define the terms of your life, and nobody else can do that for you. What does happiness and success look like for you? For every single one of us, that's something different. What may be success to Oprah Winfrey is something totally different than success for you. What was considered a success for your mother or grandmother is not the same for you today. You get to define the terms of your life. You get to say what a win is and what success looks like. For me, happiness and true success always has meant family. I want to have a family of my own so that I can bridge the gap for them financially if necessary and be the person who changes our family legacy. That has always been what my version of success looks like. Being able to use all that God has given me as far as my gifts, intellect, and formal education to be creative and becoming a full-time entrepreneur who helps others are what truly make me feel the most alive. That is what makes me feel full and complete on the inside.

I truly believe that when I'm in that place doing what it is that brings me the most joy and represents success, all of the other physical or material things will show up. All of those things will show up in their time. The beauty of it all is that even if none of the material things show up, I'm still happy and okay. I'm still content because my success was defined by having a family of my own, being able to be creative, using all that God has given me, and walking in my purpose full-time. With those things, I'm set.

Define your life not based on what others have or what you see. Define your life based on what you need to walk in the purpose that God has for your life. Define your terms of your life. Don't get caught up in the comparison trap. In the world in which we live, there is always a timeline, a Facebook or Instagram feed, or a picture. There are subliminal messages that we are receiving all throughout the day, and it is very easy to get caught in the comparison trap of looking at your life and feeling like it's not where it should be or feeling like somebody else has something better. You begin to feel that they're living this awesome life, and you're not making any progress. I want to remind you that people aren't posting their bad moments. There are very few people who are being transparent about the difficult things that life can bring you.

Every single person has the same 24 hours in a day. We often experience a lot of the same struggles and a lot of the same battles as we overcome some of the same hurdles such as insecurities, depression, past hurt, and disappointment. No matter how glamorous a life may look or appear to be, it's not. Everybody experiences bad moments. Everybody's life deals them their own set of circumstances and struggles. Please don't waste the precious decisions that you get to make throughout the course of a day because I am a big believer that people have the ability to make a certain number of well-executed thoughts and actions in a single day.

For each person that may be different. You may be able to successfully complete three to five well-thought-out, well-executed tasks a day before your brain just burns out and gets tired and frustrated. For me, I land somewhere around about seven well-executed tasks. I can make seven really good solid decisions in a day before I am either mentally or physically fatigued. Don't spend your brainpower focusing on what you don't have, but rather you should focus on what it will take to get you to where you would like to go.

Your life at its current state is right where it needs to be, and everything that you've had to experience in your past has brought you to this very moment. What you do with the future is contingent upon the actions that you start to take right now. If you find yourself spending a lot of time comparing yourself and getting down and depressed because you are not where you feel like you should be, I encourage you to take breaks and fast from social media. Spend time focusing on your path, your journey, and the place that you have to go to accomplish the things that you want to achieve. Spend your moments doing that, and I can guarantee you will start to see a shift in your life and will see things move in a different direction.

We spend a lot of time on these social outlets social platforms and give a lot of energy and resources to them, but what if you replaced the time that you spend on social media with something that actually moved the needle forward in your life? What if you focused on something that actually pushed you forward and moved you one step closer to your goals? How much farther do you think that you would be? Living life on your own terms means that you get to decide. You get to be the captain of the ship, and you get to make the decision. Define what success looks like for you and what you believe success to be and then take the steps in that direction.

One of the analogies that I typically use to describe life to is the connect-the-dots little color sheets we would do as children. There would be a whole page of dots numbered from 1 to 100, and you would have to go from dot to dot. By the time you connected all of the dots, you had a whole picture. Right now, the distance between the dots varies, so the distance to go from dot one to two may have been short but to go from dot two to dot three may have been a longer distance. The reality is you can't get from 1 to 2 or 2 to 3 if you don't start to move. You can't complete the picture unless you continually move forward no matter the distance or the route. You move forward, and then as you move all of the pieces, places, things, and people along the journey and before you leave this earth, there is a completed picture that develops. However, you can't complete the picture if you stay stuck or stand still; you have to move. Spend less time comparing and more time acting.

People-pleasing and seeking approval of others are robbers of your happiness because they will keep you from what it is that's designed for you. As we grow, evolve, change, and become the people who God has called us to be, we need less approval of others and only the approval of God to feel content and happy. You arrive at a place that what somebody thinks or feels doesn't move you, and you can finally start to make decisions that are in your best interest. Arriving at the place of being completely sure of who you are means that the approval of others is non-existent. When struggling with your own self-worth and identity, it's easy to make decisions that are not in your best interest because you want approval of others. Oftentimes, making choices like this doesn't move you forward at all. Although it may appear like it's the right thing to do, it doesn't serve you the best. It may serve some other people well. It may be great for a whole bunch of other folks who are receiving from your people-pleasing, but it doesn't move you to where you ultimately need to be. It's okay to make the choice that is best for your life to put yourself in the best position possible.

Oftentimes, people suffer from low self-esteem or from the people-pleasing to gain the approval of others. You minimize yourself, your wants, and desires. You don't speak up for yourself, and assuming that they're just going along with the flow makes you a little bit more likeable, fun to be around, and more socially acceptable. Eventually, you start to feel less appreciated and noticed, and you feel taken for granted more until you burn out. That's not fair to you, and you do an injustice to yourself when you choose to put other people's needs, wants, and desires above your own.

I remember being a 16-year-old girl who was a very active teenager in high school. I was the captain of the cheerleading squad. I was a part of almost every club and organization including the band and the drama team. I did everything that the school pretty much had to offer. I was very well-rounded and well-known around the school and made really good grades. I remember finding out that I was pregnant at 16, and I was so afraid of what people would think of me that I hid the pregnancy for as long as I possibly could. I remember still cheering at football games and feeling horrible while still tossing people in the air, kicking, and flipping. I needed to conceal the fact that I was pregnant, and I was not ready to face the level of disappointment that I thought was going to come along with my teenage pregnancy.

For many years after having my son, moving through life, and going to college, I remember still operating like the little girl who needed to show and prove to people that just because I had a child at 16, I was going to be okay. I carried around the burden of trying to gain others' approval through my accomplishments, my degree, and my business that I started. Being successful wasn't even really about me. It was just about showing the world that I'm not going to be a statistic or what they thought I was going to be. I carried around that weight, and for a very long time, I held on to the burdensome feeling that I was a teenage mother. Eventually, that weight got very heavy to the point that I made the decision to set myself free. I made the decision to start doing things that were in my best interests and not the interests of others. I put my wants and my desires first because people-pleasing and seeking approval of others is a vicious, never-ending cycle, and there's never enough that you can do to make someone love, accept, or appreciate you. There's nothing you can do to trigger that. The people who are called to be in your life accept you as you are, and those people who are designed to be there will be there.

If you feel like you're consistently overextending yourself for people and are not getting that same level of consideration back, I encourage you to just sit and think about why you make the decision to put others' interests ahead of your own. If that is just naturally who you are because you have that Mother Theresa-type energy going, go for it, and that should fulfill you. However, if you often find yourself feeling unappreciated and unvalued and if you feel like you're doing all of the giving, and people are doing all of the taking, then I encourage you to just step back for a moment and think about why is it that you put other people's interests ahead of your own. Understand that "no" is a complete sentence. It doesn't require a "but" or anything to follow it. "No" is a complete sentence, and it is totally okay for you to use it whenever you see fit.

Oftentimes I would never be the person who told anybody "no." It didn't matter how big the request was, what the time commitment was, or what I would have to sacrifice. If somebody asked me to do something, I hardly ever said "no." I actually can't even recall a moment when "no" was my response. Even if it was something that I didn't want to do, I would feel bad for saying "no." If I can be very honest and transparent, I still struggle with this today. I'm starting to become more comfortable with telling people "no," and I no longer make commitments to people that put me into strained situations. I've realized I do myself a disservice when I commit to things that I know are going to be very difficult for me to execute because it is going to cause some level of strain. If I don't want to do it, if I can't do it, or if there's a lack of resources that prevent me from being able to do it, then the answer today is simply "no." In the beginning, that's going to make the people who are used to the way that you've always behaved or the way that you've always responded extremely uncomfortable. The reality is that choosing yourself first is what you should be doing anyway.

There is nothing wrong with making the decision to make yourself the priority and make your mental health and the health of your soul and your body the priorities. The only approval that matters is the approval of God. Arriving at the place that it no longer matters what others think about what's in your heart that makes you happy is so freeing. It's so freeing when it no longer matters what anybody thinks. You don't have to feel obligated to do what somebody else wants you to do in an attempt for them to say, "Hey, that was a great job." It's so freeing on the other side of that. Walking in my purpose and doing what God has called me to do means more to me than what others will think of me and my journey.

When I first started *Overcoming Her,* people often didn't understand, and they were trying to figure out what I was doing and what its purpose was. They felt that my vision was not going anywhere. I got a lot of backlash from people who just didn't understand, and that's okay. Some people can't operate past their own level of understanding. They have to go out and seek their own understanding first about their life and the things that should be relevant and important to them before they can ever understand what it is that God has called you to do or what your life should look like. Although some people were saying to me, "Hey, you know I see what you're doing, but what is that all about? How do you think that's going to work?" I often remember and realize that what God has called me to do will always and forever mean more to me than what others think. That allows me to freely share what my life has looked like, what I have been through, and what the successes and failures of my life have been.

I remember going to my monthly life group. I have a group of women with whom I fellowship on a monthly basis, and this was my first time being a part of the group. I have struggled more recently with sharing some of what I was and am still dealing with in my life regarding the situation with my youngest son's father. I was expressing to the group how empowering it felt to know your purpose and walk in it, but there also comes with that knowledge a great weight and responsibility that you can't ever ignore. I shared with them my struggles with trying to identify if I was doing what God asked me to do. One of the other ladies in the life group shared something powerful with me. She went around the whole table and prophesied, and she hit the nail right on the head. Then, she came to me, and I was terrified at that point because I didn't know what she was going to say, but part of me was really interested. Another part of me wanted to put my fingers in my ears and say, "Oh no-no-no-no-no, I don't want to hear this. Oh no-no-no." As soon as she opened her mouth, the first thing that she said was that God was proud of me. In a matter of seconds, I begin to weep because there have been so many moments throughout my life in which I felt like I disappointed God.

There were so many times when I was like *man, you know I'm just one big mistake after mistake after mistake from being a teenage mom at the age of 16 to two failed relationships and domestic abuse.* Oh man, the list can go on and on. There were so many things that I felt like I had failed to do His way, and I felt that I disappointed God. In that moment when she said to me that He's proud of me, and I'm on the right path and just to continue to move forward because there was so much in store for me, I got the confirmation that the only approval that matters is God's approval . The only person that I seek to please today is Him. He's shown up, and He showed out in every one of my darkest seasons in my life, and when I need Him, I know He will be there. To know that I surrender my life, my plans, my hopes, and my dreams to what He has for me is completely freeing. Before you can get really clear about what it is that God has for you, you have to be sure who you are, and you have to care more about your life, your journey, and your best interests than you do about anybody else. Then, in perfect alignment, God will bring you to and through anything you need to fulfill the calling that He has for you.

Key Principle #10

Understand Yourself

There is self-love, self-esteem, and self-acceptance that I believe to be the most important "selves" that I have come to know and understand. Self-love is all about the right the actions that you take to show yourself love. How you think about yourself will determine how you will behave and treat yourself. Self-love is all about the actions that you take to show yourself love. Taking time out of your day to treat yourself well is an important part in this journey. It should be a part of your standard self-care and mental health. What are you doing to show yourself love? Oftentimes we spend so much doing for others that we forget to do for ourselves, and it is extremely important that you take time out of your day to do something for you. Treat yourself to a manicure or pedicure once a month or a massage. Go out to dinner by yourself so you can be in your own thoughts in your own moment and enjoy just being alone and being able to just be.

I remember when hiring my first life coach, I was afraid and unsure what she was going to come back with. The title of the program that I signed up for was, "I'm Single, Now What?" I was just coming out of another epically failed relationship, and I was tired. I felt like the program spoke directly to me. At the time, I was not in a position financially to invest into life culture, but I knew that it was extremely important for my mental health that I do something for myself that was going to improve me. Therefore, I made the sacrifice and decision to hire her and to take seriously the work required to change my life. That investment into myself was me showing myself some love. That invested reflected me saying, "Hey Simone, it's important that you do something for yourself that makes you a better person that heals you from that poor decision-making cycle that you've been experiencing in your life. Self-love for me was all about putting into action something that could bear some type of positive fruit in my life.

Self-esteem deals with what and how you think about yourself. The way that you think about yourself ultimately shapes the way that you walk, talk, and move. It also plays a major part in what you attract into your life and the places and the things you find interesting. Before understanding who I was and what God called me to be, I often would think that I wasn't good enough; that's truly what I thought about myself. I wasn't good enough for love. I wasn't good enough for anyone to want to stay in my life like friends or relationships. Because I thought that way, it allowed me to accept anything that anybody was willing to offer. I had no standard because I just I wanted to just have somebody or something there to show some type of compassion or love towards me. I literally accepted anything.

On the outside, people thought that I had self-esteem that was through the roof. They would think that I had it all figured out and that I knew all about who I was and what I wanted. They believed that I had a level of boldness and presence, and that may have been what the exterior looked like, but on the inside, I was the most unsure, uncertain, and approval-seeking person. I wanted to hear someone tell me that he or she loved me or that he or she thought I did a good job, and I would take that from anyone who would give that affirmation to me. Because of that, I often ended up in relationships, friendships, and situations with people with whom I had no business. I entertained people who weren't even qualified to sit in the same room as me because I knew that I was different, and God placed me here for a reason. Even though I wasn't quite sure what that reason was the whole time, I knew that there was something.

When you have a purpose that is grand, not everybody should have access to you. Not everybody should be able to have access to you to be able to affect your energy, thoughts, mind, or mindset. You have to guard your peace; you have to guard your mind, heart, and your spirit from things that don't serve you. The place that God has called you to go, the people that He has called you to be around, and the purpose that He has for you will require with every bone and breath of air in your body.

When you have low self-esteem, you're grabbing at the first sign of anything that you could potentially think is going to satisfy you or give you a certain type of feeling or emotion. Making choices and decisions based on feelings is a very dangerous thing to do. You have to set a standard for the way that you think about yourself and the way that you view your self-esteem. You have to have a basis in which you are going to determine what's allowed and what's not allowed to occupy space in your life. In the moment that the things that are not good for you try to show up in your life, remove yourself, and you will find contentment and peace in removing yourself.

Self-acceptance it's accepting who you are flaws and all. Making the decision to accept yourself in every single part of your character that makes you unique is so freeing. Not feeling the need to change who you are to satisfy other people, being true to yourself, owning exactly who you are, and accepting it is essential. I often make very quick decisions, and this is in every area of my life. If I decide that I'm going to do it, or I'm going to achieve it, then I run full steam ahead in that direction. If I decide to get into a relationship, that decision is pretty quick, and when I'm done, and I decide to be done, I'm usually done pretty quickly too. I make quick decisions. Now, either these quick decisions can lead to a positive outcome or sometimes, they can lead to a negative one. Even if the outcome is not the most positive one, there's still a lesson or something that I can take away. People often judge me for this. They often tell me, "Oh man, Simone, you move too fast. You need to slow down. You need to just sit still." I used to try to change this about myself. Along the way, I associated making quick decisions with being a bad thing or negative thing. The reality is that my ability to make quick decisions has served me in so many ways. It has helped me in so many ways. The average person typically sits on a decision. They don't take any action towards a resolution, and they don't move forward. I don't ever suffer from that because I make a decision, and I move on it. I move forward, and it's always very interesting that when people are giving out their opinions or their assessments of who you are and the choices that you've made, it's always very interesting that depending upon how that decision benefits them, they decide if they're okay with it or if it's something that you should change about yourself.

My ability to make quick decisions is always a great thing when I'm making a decision that would rescue a person out of his or her tough spot. An example would begetting on the phone and talking to the loan company and coming to a negotiated settlement so that they don't foreclose on your house. I have the ability to move quickly and jump right in and make a quick decisions to solve your problem. In an example like that, is a great quality to have. However, when the quick decision results in maybe some disappointment or heartbreak, even then it's "Oh Simone, you move too fast. You shouldn't make decisions so quickly; you need to slow down." That's why self-acceptance is so important because you have to learn to accept who you are flaws and all, experiences and all. Every journey and lesson that life has had to teach you played a major part in God moving you in the direction that He needed you to go so He can mold and craft you you into the person that He wants you to be. Finally, after we've committed to the process, seen it through, done the work, and loved and accepted ourselves, we arrive at a place of peace. Peace is where the majority of us aspire to spend the bulk of our time.

Happiness is an inside job. Never give anyone else the responsibility for your happiness. Ultimate peace comes when you understand that you are the sole owner of your happiness. People, situations, and circumstances change. How you react to the change is a large part of how the outcome will turn out. Make the decision to be positive and look at life as the glass being half full versus half empty even when everything is not perfect still.

Happiness is on you, and the perspective through which you look at situations is also important. Happiness is truly an inside job, and if you are constantly seeking others to make you happy or to dictate how you feel in the day or in the moment, you are setting yourself up for grave disappointment. Oftentimes, I would look for my happiness in other people. To be honest with you, I didn't even really know what made me happy. I just knew that if I did something for somebody else, and it made them feel happy, I felt like I did something right. I often searched for my happiness in life and in the approval of others.

Even in the relationship with my youngest son's father, I remember making decisions to continue in the relationship and to attempt being a family living together without being married because I thought that got me a little bit closer to happiness. Remember, I shared with you what my definition of success was, and success for me has always been having a family of my own. Although I had an unplanned pregnancy, I still remember hoping and praying that it would turn into a family of my own, and that it would bring me some supreme level of happiness. I remember crying many nights when it wasn't turning out that way. I remember feeling down and frustrated because I was seeking for this other person to make me feel whole, complete, and happy. Then, it clicked. I went back to the basics. I remembered what I learned in my own life coaching and my own reflection. I remembered how I make decisions and what I continue to help women deal with on a day-to-day basis. I realized that I had to stop making decisions out of my feelings. Feelings change way too quickly for you to ever just make decisions based on them.

I started making logical decisions based on facts, not on emotions which allowed me to set myself free. That allowed me to go back to what it was that God called me to do, and I became 100% okay if that relationship never turned into marriage. This shift in my thoughts occurred because I was not looking for my happiness in this other person. I took my power and control back. I took back the driving wheel to my life and my destiny. I realized that happiness will only show up when I continue to do what it is that I know that I've been called to do, and that's nobody else's responsibility but my own.

I vowed to myself after making it through yet another heartbreak that I was done making decisions based on emotions. I was done giving somebody else the responsibility of my life. I was going to own every single piece of that. I would focus on facts and logic and make decisions from a very logical place. Life ultimately will bring you obstacles and challenges. There will be things that you have to overcome, but you can have peace knowing that everything is designed to mold you and move you. Learning to dance even when the rain is pouring can provide you with calmness. Understand that it will not last forever, and inner peace should give you the ability to navigate whatever circumstances you face.

How do you find that inner peace and calmness? Whenever I'm anxious or in a moment of unrest and uncertainty, I stop. I breathe, close my eyes, get very still, and meditate for a moment. I change my focus. Whatever it is that's causing the anxiety, I'll go and do something else, and then I come back to it later. I've learned to dance even in the rain because even once you arrive at your why, understand your purpose, fulfill it, and try with everything in your might to fulfill the assignment, that still does not mean that there won't be challenges. That does not mean that obstacles won't come. Sometimes, you just have to find the beauty in the struggle. Find the beauty in whatever situation you are experiencing. Learn the lesson and then move forward.

In understanding key principle number 10, know that gaining peace in life means understanding that when the difficult moments show up, it's not the end. It is just another page in your book of life.

If you are ready to understand your life's experiences on a deeper level

and turn Obstacles into Opportunities visit

www.SimoneAdrianne.com

for your FREE Life + Business Bundle that will include:

- 7-Steps to Self-Actualization Workbook
- 3 Part Video Series
- Quickstart Business Checklist

Are you tired of feeling stuck, Unsure about your life, and Confused about the purpose that God has for you?

If you have ever wondered or asked the questions, "Why you? Why does life seem so difficult and why do obstacles keep finding their way directly to you?"

Maybe it's a loss of a loved one, disappointment from your childhood, insecurities, guilt, or heartbreak. Do you often feel like you keep taking the same test in life and failing it?

You know there is more that you desire, but you just can't seem to Overcome.

Well, that is all about to change. You're about to experience a shift and learn to take Obstacles and turn them into Opportunities. Take all the experiences life has provided you and use them to become unstoppable.

Simone Adrianne will show you how.

Simone knows all too well about life's hardships. She became a single mother at 16 when her son's father passed away in a fatal car accident. She thought she had found the happily ever after at 19 and got engaged only to end up in a domestically violent relationship that she had to walk away from to save her life and her son's life. Months later, she found herself in the middle of a legal battle in which she was fighting for her freedom.

Through it all, Simone refused to quit on herself and the life that she envisioned. Now, as the Founder of *Overcoming Her*,

SIMONE ADRIANNE

she is a speaker, life and business coach, and mentor to women all over the world, Simone writes candidly about what occurred in her past, what she had to learn, and how she got out of her own way and she wants to help you. In this book, Simone will provide you with a blueprint that will guide you to:

* Deal with your past

* Understand your value

* Execute in the areas of life that you want to change

*Arrive at place of self-actualization and wholeness

Let Simone's personal stories and insight empower you to leave behind your old way of thinking and truly step into all that is waiting for you!

About the Author

Simone Adrianne is a businesswoman, author, and certified life coach who balances career, faith, and family. She has been the driving force behind many successful brand launches including her own and has made it her mission in life to serve others. Her desire is to provide them with real tools and resources to overcome any of their life's challenges and turn those very obstacles into opportunities to make an impact with books, events, and coaching programs. Simone has a Bachelor's Degree in Business Administration with a concentration in Marketing and a Master's Degree in Business Administration with a focus in International Business. She currently resides in Houston, TX with her husband and two amazing boys, and she is also very active in her local community.

www.ingramcontent.com/pod-product-compliance
Lightning Source LLC
Chambersburg PA
CBHW021844090426
42811CB00033B/2134/J